GRADUATION

MAYA ANGELOU

LOOKING FORWARD

"Graduation" is a chapter from Maya Angelou's largely autobiographical book *I Know Why the Caged Bird Sings*. As is usually the case with most graduation tales, this account focuses on growing up. With greater intensity than ever before, the narrator of the story is confronted with the fact that she is black. A surprising twist to the graduation ceremony helps her see what that fact means to her.

WORDS TO WATCH FOR

Below is a list of words which may be unfamiliar to you. Before reading "Graduation," check the list and be sure that you understand the meaning of each word.

purported – claimed; alleged
piqued – offended or insulted; irritated
meticulous – exact; precise; accurate
palpable – obvious; evident
elocution – speaking style and skill

Copyright 1990. Perfection Learning Corporation, Logan, Iowa 51546

19 20 21 22 23 24 PP 18 17 16 15 14 13

The children in Stamps[1] trembled visibly with anticipation. Some adults were excited too, but to be certain the whole young population had come down with graduation epidemic. Large classes were graduating from both the grammar school and the high school. Even those who were years removed from their own day of glorious release were anxious to help with preparations as a kind of dry run. The junior students who were moving into the vacating classes' chairs were tradition-bound to show their talents for leadership and management. They strutted through the school and around the campus exerting pressure on the lower grades. Their authority was so new that occasionally if they pressed a little too hard it had to be overlooked. After all, next term was coming, and it never hurt a sixth grader to have a play sister in the eighth grade, or a tenth-year student to be able to call a twelfth

---

[1]Stamps is a small town in Arkansas.

grader Bubba. So all was endured in a spirit of shared understanding. But the graduating classes themselves were the nobility. Like travelers with exotic destinations on their minds, the graduates were remarkably forgetful. They came to school without their books, or tablets or even pencils. Volunteers fell over themselves to secure replacements for the missing equipment. When accepted, the willing workers might or might not be thanked, and it was of no importance to the pregraduation rites. Even teachers were respectful of the now quiet and aging seniors, and tended to speak to them, if not as equals, as beings only slightly lower than themselves. After tests were returned and grades given, the student body, which acted like an extended family, knew who did well, who excelled, and what piteous ones had failed.

Unlike the white high school, Lafayette County Training School distinguished itself by having neither lawn, nor hedges, nor tennis court, nor climbing ivy. Its two buildings (main classrooms, the grade school and home economics) were set on a dirt hill with no fence to limit either its boundaries or those of bordering farms. There was a large expanse to the left of the school which was used alternately as a baseball diamond or basketball court. Rusty hoops on swaying poles represented the permanent recreational equipment, although bats and balls could be borrowed from the P. E. teacher if the borrower was qualified and if the diamond wasn't occupied.

Over this rocky area relieved by a few shady tall persimmon trees the graduating class walked. The girls often held hands and no longer bothered to speak to the lower students. There was a sadness about them, as if this old world was not their home and they were bound for higher ground. The boys, on the other hand, had become more friendly, more outgoing. A decided change from the closed attitude they projected while studying for finals. Now they seemed not ready to give up the old school, the familiar paths and classrooms. Only a small percentage would be continuing on to college — one of the South's A & M (agricultural and mechanical) schools, which trained Negro youths to be carpenters, farmers, handymen, masons, maids, cooks and baby nurses. Their future rode heavily on their shoulders, and blinded them to the collective joy that had pervaded the lives of the boys and girls in the grammar school graduating class.

Parents who could afford it had ordered new shoes and ready-made clothes for themselves from Sears and Roebuck or Montgomery Ward. They also engaged the best seamstresses to make the floating graduating dresses and to cut down second-hand pants which would be pressed to a military slickness for the important event.

Oh, it was important, all right. Whitefolks would attend the ceremony, and two or three would speak of God and home, and the Southern way of life, and Mrs. Parsons, the principal's wife, would play the graduation march while the lower-grade graduates paraded down the aisles and took their seats below the platform. The high school seniors would wait in empty classrooms to make their dramatic entrance.

In the Store I was the person of the moment. The birthday girl. The center. Bailey[2] had graduated the year before, although to do so he had had to forfeit all pleasures to make up for his time lost in Baton Rouge.

My class was wearing butter-yellow piqué[3] dresses, and Momma launched out on mine. She smocked the yoke into tiny crisscrossing puckers, then shirred the rest of the bodice. Her dark fingers ducked in and out of the lemo-

[2]Bailey is the narrator's brother.
[3]Piqué is a very durable fabric made of cotton, silk, or rayon.

ny cloth as she embroidered raised daisies around the hem. Before she considered herself finished she had added a crocheted cuff on the puff sleeves, and a pointy crocheted collar.

I was going to be lovely. A walking model of all the various styles of fine hand sewing and it didn't worry me that I was only twelve years old and merely graduating from the eighth grade. Besides, many teachers in Arkansas Negro schools had only that diploma and were licensed to impart wisdom.

The days had become longer and more noticeable. The faded beige of former times had been replaced with strong and sure colors. I began to see my classmates' clothes, their skin tones, and the dust that waved off pussy willows. Clouds that lazed across the sky were objects of great concern to me. Their shiftier shapes might have held a message that in my new happiness and with a little bit of time I'd soon decipher. During that period I looked at the arch of heaven so religiously my neck kept a steady ache. I had taken to smiling more often, and my jaws hurt from the unaccustomed activity. Between the two physical sore spots, I suppose I could have been uncomfortable, but that was not the case. As a member of the winning team (the graduating class of

1940) I had outdistanced unpleasant sensations by miles. I was headed for the freedom of open fields.

Youth and social approval allied themselves with me and we trammeled memories of slights and insults. The wind of our swift passage remodeled my features. Lost tears were pounded to mud and then to dust. Years of withdrawal were brushed aside and left behind, as hanging ropes of parasitic moss.

My work alone had awarded me a top place and I was going to be one of the first called in the graduating ceremonies. On the classroom blackboard, as well as on the bulletin board in the auditorium, there were blue stars and white stars and red stars. No absences, no tardinesses, and my academic work was among the best of the year. I could say the preamble to the Constitution even faster than Bailey. We timed ourselves often: "Wethepeopleofthe UnitedStatesinordertoformamoreperfect union. . ." I had memorized the Presidents of the United States from Washington to Roosevelt in chronological as well as alphabetical order.

My hair pleased me too. Gradually the black mass had lengthened and thickened, so that it kept at last to its braided pattern, and I didn't have to yank my scalp off when I tried to comb it.

Louise and I had rehearsed the exercises until we tired out ourselves. Henry Reed was class valedictorian[4] He was a small, very black boy with hooded eyes, a long, broad nose and an oddly shaped head. I had admired him for years because each term he and I vied for the best grades in our class. Most often he bested me, but instead of being disappointed I was pleased that we shared top places between us. Like many Southern Black children, he lived with his grandmother, who was as strict as Momma and as kind as she knew how to be. He was courteous, respectful and soft-spoken to elders, but on the playground he chose to play the roughest games. I admired him. Anyone, I reckoned, sufficiently afraid or sufficiently dull could be polite. But to be able to operate at a top level with both adults and children was admirable.

His valedictory speech was entitled "To Be or Not to Be."[5] The rigid tenth-grade teacher had helped him write it. He'd been working on the dramatic stresses for months.

---

[4] A valedictorian is the student who has earned the highest overall grade-point average.
[5] "To Be or Not to Be" is a famous soliloquy spoken by Hamlet in Shakespeare's play *Hamlet*.

The weeks until graduation were filled with heady activities. A group of small children were to be presented in a play about buttercups and daisies and bunny rabbits. They could be heard throughout the building practicing their hops and their little songs that sounded like silver bells. The older girls (nongraduates, of course) were assigned the task of making refreshments for the night's festivities. A tangy scent of ginger, cinnamon, nutmeg and chocolate wafted around the home economics building as the budding cooks made samples for themselves and their teachers.

In every corner of the workshop, axes and saws split fresh timber as the woodshop boys made sets and stage scenery. Only the graduates were left out of the general bustle. We were free to sit in the library at the back of the building or look in quite detachedly, naturally, on the measures being taken for our event.

Even the minister preached on graduation the Sunday before. His subject was, "Let your light so shine that men will see your good works and praise your Father, Who is in Heaven." Although the sermon was purported to be addressed to us, he used the occasion to speak to backsliders, gamblers and general ne'er-do-wells. But since he had called our names at the beginning of the service we were mollified.

Among Negroes the tradition was to give presents to children going only from one grade to another. How much more important this was when the person was graduating at the top of the class. Uncle Willie and Momma had sent away for a Mickey Mouse watch like Bailey's. Louise gave me four embroidered handkerchiefs. (I gave her crocheted doilies.) Mrs. Sneed, the minister's wife, made me an undershirt to wear for graduation, and nearly every customer gave me a nickel or maybe even a dime with the instruction "Keep on moving to higher ground," or some such encouragement.

Amazingly the great day finally dawned and I was out of bed before I knew it. I threw open the back door to see it more clearly, but Momma said, "Sister, come away from that door and put your robe on."

I hoped the memory of that morning would never leave me. Sunlight was itself young, and the day had none of the insistence maturity would bring it in a few hours. In my robe and barefoot in the backyard, under cover of going to see about my new beans, I gave myself up to the gentle warmth and thanked God that no matter what evil I had done in my life He had allowed me to live to see this day. Somewhere in my fatalism I had expected to die, accidentally, and never have the chance to walk up the stairs in the auditorium and gracefully receive my hard-earned diploma. Out of God's merciful bosom I had won reprieve.

Bailey came out in his robe and gave me a box wrapped in Christmas paper. He said he had saved his money for months to pay for it. It felt like a box of chocolates, but I knew Bailey wouldn't save money to buy candy when we had all we could want under our noses.

He was as proud of the gift as I. It was a soft-leather-bound copy of a collection of poems by Edgar Allan Poe, or, as Bailey and I called him, "Eap." I turned to "Annabel Lee" and we walked up and down the garden rows, the cool dirt between our toes, reciting the beautifully sad lines.[6]

Momma made a Sunday breakfast although it was only Friday. After we finished the blessing, I opened my eyes to find the watch on my plate. It was a dream of a day. Everything went smoothly and to my credit. I didn't have to be reminded or scolded for anything. Near evening I was too jittery to attend to chores, so

---

[6]Edgar Allan Poe, a famous nineteenth-century American short story writer, also created haunting poems such as "Annabel Lee."

Bailey volunteered to do all before his bath.

Days before, we had made a sign for the Store, and as we turned out the lights Momma hung the cardboard over the doorknob. It read clearly: CLOSED, GRADUATION.

My dress fitted perfectly and everyone said that I looked like a sunbeam in it. On the hill, going toward the school, Bailey walked behind with Uncle Willie, who muttered, "Go on, Ju." He wanted him to walk ahead with us because it embarrassed him to have to walk so slowly. Bailey said he'd let the ladies walk together, and the men would bring up the rear. We all laughed, nicely.

Little children dashed by out of the dark like fireflies. Their crepe-paper dresses and butterfly wings were not made for running and we heard more than one rip, dryly, and the regretful "uh uh" that followed.

The school blazed without gaiety. The windows seemed cold and unfriendly from the lower hill. A sense of ill-fated timing crept over me, and if Momma hadn't reached for my hand I would have drifted back to Bailey and Uncle Willie, and possibly beyond. She made a few slow jokes about my feet getting cold, and tugged me along to the now-strange building.

Around the front steps, assurance came

back. There were my fellow "greats," the graduating class. Hair brushed back, legs oiled, new dresses and pressed pleats, fresh pocket handkerchiefs and little handbags, all homesewn. Oh, we were up to snuff, all right. I joined my comrades and didn't even see my family go in to find seats in the crowded auditorium.

The school band struck up a march and all classes filed in as had been rehearsed. We stood in front of our seats, as assigned, and on a signal from the choir director, we sat. No sooner had this been accomplished than the band started to play the national anthem. We rose again and sang the song, after which we recited the pledge of allegiance. We remained standing for a brief minute before the choir director and the principal signaled to us, rather desperately I thought, to take our seats. The command was so unusual that our carefully rehearsed and smooth-running machine was thrown off. For a full minute we fumbled for our chairs and bumped into each other awkwardly. Habits change or solidify under pressure, so in our state of nervous tension we had been ready to follow our usual assembly pattern: the American national anthem, then the pledge of allegiance, then the song every Black person I knew called the Negro National

Anthem. All done in the same key, with the same passion and most often standing on the same foot.

Finding my seat at last, I was overcome with a presentiment of worse things to come. Something unrehearsed, unplanned, was going to happen, and we were going to be made to look bad. I distinctly remember being explicit in the choice of pronoun. It was "we," the graduating class, the unit, that concerned me then.

The principal welcomed "parents and friends" and asked the Baptist minister to lead us in prayer. His invocation was brief and punchy, and for a second I thought we were getting on the high road to right action. When the principal came back to the dais, however, his voice had changed. Sounds always affected me profoundly and the principal's voice was one of my favorites. During assembly it melted and lowed weakly into the audience. It had not been in my plan to listen to him, but my curiosity was piqued and I straightened up to give him my attention.

He was talking about Booker T. Washington,[7] our "late great leader," who said we can be as close as the fingers on the hand, etc. . . . Then he said a few vague things about friendship and the friendship of kindly people to those less fortunate than themselves. With that his voice nearly faded, thin, away. Like a river diminishing to a stream and then to a trickle. But he cleared his throat and said, "Our speaker tonight, who is also our friend, came from Texarkana to deliver the commencement address, but due to the irregularity of the train schedule, he's going to, as they say, 'speak and run.' " He said that we understood and wanted the man to know that we were most grateful for the time he was able to give us and then something about how we were willing always to adjust to another's program, and without more ado — "I give you Mr. Edward Donleavy."

Not one but two white men came through the door off-stage. The shorter one walked to the speaker's platform, and the tall one moved to the center seat and sat down. But that was our principal's seat, and already occupied. The dislodged gentleman bounced around for a long breath or two before the Baptist minister gave him his chair, then with more dignity than the situation deserved, the minister walked off the stage.

Donleavy looked at the audience once (on reflection, I'm sure that he wanted only to reassure himself that we were really there), adjust-

---

[7]Booker T. Washington was a famous black educator and leader.

ed his glasses and began to read from a sheaf of papers.

He was glad "to be here and to see the work going on just as it was in the other schools."

At the first "Amen" from the audience I willed the offender to immediate death by choking on the word. But Amens and Yes, sir's began to fall around the room like rain through a ragged umbrella.

He told us of the wonderful changes we children in Stamps had in store. The Central School (naturally, the white school was Central) had already been granted improvements that would be in use in the fall. A well-known artist was coming from Little Rock to teach art to them. They were going to have the newest microscopes and chemistry equipment for their laboratory. Mr. Donleavy didn't leave us long in the dark over who made these improvements available to Central High. Nor were we to be ignored in the general betterment scheme he had in mind.

He said that he had pointed out to people at a very high level that one of the first-line football tacklers at Arkansas Agricultural and Mechanical College had graduated from good old Lafayette County Training School. Here fewer Amen's were heard. Those few that did break through lay dully in the air with the heaviness of habit.

He went on to praise us. He went on to say how he had bragged that "one of the best basketball players at Fisk[8] sank his first ball right here at Lafayette County Training School."

The white kids were going to have a chance to become Galileos and Madame Curies and Edisons and Gauguins, and our boys (the girls weren't even in on it) would try to be Jesse Owenses and Joe Louises.[9]

Owens and the Brown Bomber were great heroes in our world, but what school official in the white-golddom of Little Rock had the right to decide that those two men must be our only heroes? Who decided that for Henry Reed to become a scientist he had to work like George Washington Carver,[10] as a bootblack, to buy a lousy microscope? Bailey was obviously always going to be too small to be an athlete, so which concrete angel glued to what country seat had decided that if my brother wanted to become a lawyer he had to first pay penance for his skin

---

[8]Fisk is a prestigious university in Nashville, Tennessee, founded in 1865 for the education of blacks.
[9]Galileo was a famous Italian inventor and astronomer; the Polish Marie Curie, the discoverer of radium; Thomas Edison, the American inventor of the phonograph and light bulb; and Paul Gauguin, a brilliant French Impressionist. All were whites. Jesse Owens was a world record-setting track star and Joe Louis (also known as the Brown Bomber) was a legendary heavyweight fighter. Both were black Americans.

by picking cotton and hoeing corn and studying correspondence books at night for twenty years?

The man's dead words fell like bricks around the auditorium and too many settled in my belly. Constrained by hard-learned manners I couldn't look behind me, but to my left and right the proud graduating class of 1940 had dropped their heads. Every girl in my row had found something new to do with her handkerchief. Some folded the tiny squares into love knots, some into triangles, but most were wadding them, then pressing them flat on their yellow laps.

On the dais, the ancient tragedy was being replayed. Professor Parsons sat, a sculptor's reject, rigid. His large, heavy body seemed devoid of will or willingness, and his eyes said he was no longer with us. The other teachers examined the flag (which was draped stage right) or their notes, or the windows which opened on our now-famous playing diamond.

Graduation, the hush-hush magic time of frills and gifts and congratulations and diplomas, was finished for me before my name was called. The accomplishment was nothing. The meticulous maps, drawn in three colors of ink,

---

[10]Carver was an internationally renowned black botanist and researcher.

learning and spelling decasyllabic words, memorizing the whole of *The Rape of Lucrece*[11] — it was for nothing. Donleavy had exposed us.

We were maids and farmers, handymen and washerwomen, and anything higher that we aspired to was farcical and presumptuous.

Then I wished that Gabriel Prosser and Nat Turner had killed all whitefolks in their beds and that Abraham Lincoln had been assassinated before the signing of the Emancipation Proclamation, and that Harriet Tubman had been killed by that blow on her head and Christopher Columbus had drowned in the *Santa Maria*.[12]

It was awful to be a Negro and have no control over my life. It was brutal to be young and already trained to sit quietly and listen to charges brought against my color with no chance of defense. We should all be dead. I thought I should like to see us all dead, one on top of the other. A pyramid of flesh with the whitefolks on the bottom, as the broad base, then the Indians with their silly tomahawks and teepees and wigwams and treaties, the Negroes with their mops and recipes and cot-

[11]The long poem *The Rape of Lucrece* is by Shakespeare.
[12]President Lincoln freed most slaves with the Emancipation Proclamation; Prosser, Turner, and Tubman were blacks who fought against slavery. Christopher Columbus led the wave of European invaders to America by "discovering" the country.

ton sacks and spirituals sticking out of their mouths. The Dutch children should all stumble in their wooden shoes and break their necks. The French should choke to death on the Louisiana Purchase (1803) while silkworms ate all the Chinese with their stupid pigtails. As a species, we were an abomination. All of us.

Donleavy was running for election, and assured our parents that if he won we could count on having the only colored paved playing field in that part of Arkansas.

Also — he never looked up to acknowledge the grunts of acceptance — also, we were bound to get some new equipment for the home economics building and the workshop.

He finished, and since there was no need to give any more than the most perfunctory thank-you's, he nodded to the men on the stage, and the tall white man who was never introduced joined him at the door. They left with the attitude that now they were off to something really important. (The graduation ceremonies at Lafayette County Training School had been a mere preliminary.)

The ugliness they left was palpable. An uninvited guest who wouldn't leave. The choir was summoned and sang a modern arrangement of "Onward, Christian Soldiers," with new words pertaining to graduates seeking their place in the world. But it didn't work. Elouise, the daughter of the Baptist minister, recited "Invictus,"[13] and I could have cried at the impertinence of "I am the master of my fate, I am the captain of my soul."

My name had lost its ring of familiarity and I had to be nudged to go and receive my diploma. All my preparations had fled. I neither marched up to the stage like a conquering Amazon,[14] nor did I look in the audience for Bailey's nod of approval. Marguerite Johnson, I heard the name again, my honors were read, there were noises in the audience of appreciation, and I took my place on the stage as rehearsed.

I thought about colors I hated: ecru, puce, lavender, beige and black.

There was shuffling and rustling around me, then Henry Reed was giving his valedictory address, "To Be or Not to Be." Hadn't he heard the whitefolks? We couldn't *be,* so the question was a waste of time. Henry's voice came out clear and strong. I feared to look at him. Hadn't he got the message? There was no "nobler in the mind" for Negroes because the world didn't

---

[13]In the poem "Invictus," by William Ernest Henley, the poet declares that no matter what the situation, he controls his fate.

[14]Amazons were a legendary race of proud female warriors.

think we had minds, and they let us know it. "Outrageous fortune"? Now, that was a joke. When the ceremony was over I had to tell Henry Reed some things. That is, if I still cared. Not "rub," Henry, "erase." "Ah, there's the erase." Us.

Henry had been a good student in elocution. His voice rose on tides of promise and fell on waves of warnings. The English teacher had helped him to create a sermon winging through Haplet's soliloquy. To be a man, a doer, a builder, a leader, or to be a tool, an unfunny joke, a crusher of funky toadstools. I marveled that Henry could go through with the speech as if we had a choice.

I had been listening and silently rebutting each sentence with my eyes closed; then there was a hush, which in an audience warns that something unplanned is happening. I looked up and saw Henry Reed, the conservative, the proper, the A student, turn his back to the audience and turn to us (the proud graduating class of 1940) and sing, nearly speaking,

> "Lift ev'ry voice and sing
> Till earth and heaven ring
> Ring with the harmonies of Liberty. . ."

It was the poem written by James Weldon

Johnson. It was the music composed by J. Rosamond Johnson. It was the Negro national anthem. Out of habit we were singing it.

Our mothers and fathers stood in the dark hall and joined the hymn of encouragement. A kindergarten teacher led the small children onto the stage and the buttercups and daisies and bunny rabbits marked time and tried to follow:

"Stony the road we trod
Bitter the chastening rod
Felt in the days when hope, unborn, had
  died.
Yet with a steady beat
Have not our weary feet
Come to the place for which our fathers
  sighed?"

Every child I knew had learned that song with his ABC's and along with "Jesus Loves Me This I Know." But I personally had never heard it before. Never heard the words, despite the thousands of times I had sung them. Never thought they had anything to do with me.

On the other hand, the words of Patrick

Henry had made such an impression on me that I had been able to stretch myself tall and trembling and say, "I know not what course others may take, but as for me, give me liberty or give me death."

And now I heard, really for the first time:

"We have come over a way that with tears has been watered,
We have come, treading our path through the blood of the slaughtered."

While echoes of the song shivered in the air, Henry Reed bowed his head, said "Thank you," and returned to his place in the line. The tears that slipped down many faces were not wiped away in shame.

We were on top again. As always, again. We survived. The depths had been icy and dark, but now a bright sun spoke to our souls. I was no longer simply a member of the proud graduating class of 1940; I was a proud member of the wonderful, beautiful Negro race.

Oh, Black known and unknown poets, how often have your auctioned pains sustained us? Who will compute the lonely nights made less lonely by your songs, or by the empty pots made less tragic by your tales?

If we were a people much given to revealing

secrets, we might raise monuments and sacrifice to the memories of our poets, but slavery cured us of that weakness. It may be enough, however, to have it said that we survive in exact relationship to the dedication of our poets (include preachers, musicians and blues singers).

I. THE STORY LINE

A. Digging for Facts

1. Among both adults and students, graduation brings all but which of these emotions: (a) excitement, (b) pride, (c) serenity.

2. Marguerite's place at graduation (a) is one of the first since she is such a good student, (b) is changed because she cannot afford a new dress, (c) is directly after her brother Bailey's.

3. Which of the following is not one of Marguerite's graduation gifts: (a) a Mickey Mouse watch, (b) a book of Edgar Allan Poe poetry, (c) a box of candy.

4. When the Negro National Anthem is omitted, Marguerite (a) reminds the principal that they've forgotten it, (b) has a feeling something disastrous is going to occur, (c) turns to Henry and smiles.

5. Which of the following is not true about Edward Donleavy, the speaker: (a) he's president of Fisk University, (b) he's a white politician, (c) he's not well received by the audience.

6. From Donleavy's speech, Marguerite infers that he believes (a) blacks are well on the way to achieving equality, (b) whites are supposed to be the creators and blacks the athletes, (c) whites fear the future is in the hands of the blacks.

7. As a result of Donleavy's speech, Marguerite concludes that she (a) has no control over her life, (b) will go to college, (c) is sorry to be graduating.

8. Marguerite objects to Henry's speech because she thinks (a) Henry is bragging about his learning, (b) she should be giving the speech instead, (c) blacks have no chance "to be."

9. After Henry has the students sing the Negro National Anthem, Marguerite feels (a) proud of her heritage, (b) increasingly resentful towards whites, (c) confused about her own goals.

10. Marguerite thinks black people owe much to (a) their poets, (b) honest white politicians, (c) great black athletes.

B. Probing for Theme

Read the three statements below. Which one best captures the theme of "Graduation"?

1. Freedom begins with pride in the heart.

2. Graduation is the beginning of the rest of your life.

3. If there's a song in your heart, sing it.

II. IN SEARCH OF MEANING

1. What does Angelou mean when she writes, "On the dais, the ancient tragedy was being replayed"? How does Angelou illustrate and highlight the tragedy? Besides the tragedy referred to, what else is tragic about the moment? Do you think Marguerite overreacts to this event, or are her feelings justified? Explain.

2. Marguerite says, "I could have cried at the impertinence of 'I am the master of my fate, I am the captain of my soul.' " What do you think Henley meant when he wrote the verse? What does "Invictus" mean to Marguerite? Compare her reac-

tion to this verse to her reaction to the Negro National Anthem. How do the two poems differ, and why do Marguerite's feelings about the poems differ?

3. Analyze the plot of "Graduation." First, map the plot in terms of peaks (happiness), valleys (depression or desperation), and plains (neither extreme). Then examine how Angelou uses anticipation and surprise to keep the plot rising and falling. Finally, decide if the ending seems an artificial peak or an appropriate conclusion. Explain your responses.

4. What conflicts does Marguerite face in this selection? Which conflicts are internal, which external, and which a combination of both? Of all the conflicts, which is the hardest one for her to overcome? Give evidence for your opinions.

5. Why do you think the Negro National Anthem is omitted at the beginning of the program? What effect does the omission have on Marguerite and the rest of the audience? What is the effect on Marguerite when the anthem is finally sung? Why does it have that effect? Does it have the same effect on you? Why or

why not? How might your reaction have differed if Angelou had not included words to the anthem in her story? Explain.

III. DEVELOPING WORD POWER

Exercise A

Each of the following vocabulary words appears in a sentence taken from the story. Read the sentence, then choose the correct meaning.

1. mollified

   "But since he had called our names at the beginning of the service we were *mollified*."

   a. horrified   c. informed
   b. perplexed   d. soothed

2. vied

"I had admired him for years because each term he and I *vied* for the best grades in our class."

a. desired   c. defeated
b. competed   d. studied

3. presumptuous

"We were maids and farmers, handymen and washerwomen, and anything higher that we aspired to was farcical and *presumptuous*."

a. overbold   c. distasteful
b. absurd   d. overwhelming

4. constrained

"*Constrained* by hard-learned manners I couldn't look behind me. . ."

a. repressed   c. irritated
b. comforted   d. convinced

5. presentiment

"Finding my seat at last, I was overcome with a *presentiment* of worse things to come."

a. picture   c. expectation
b. message   d. threat

Exercise B

Select the word from the vocabulary list that best completes each sentence.

a. constrained   f. piqued
b. elocution   g. presentiment
c. meticulous   h. presumptous
d. mollified   i. purported
e. palpable   j. vied

1. The man was _?_ to be an expert on Chinese painting, but I thought he wasn't as knowledgeable as people said.

2. The referee's call _?_ Marsha, and she angrily muttered to herself as she returned to the bench.

3. Eddie was neat and _?_, but his friend Jordan never put anything away.

4. Nikki's depression was so deep, it cast a _?_ gloom over the room.

5. Ravi felt like taking his shoes off, but the presence of his grandparents _?_ him.

6. When Mark was in a bad mood, he could usually be _?_ by listening to his favorite album.

7. I had a _?_ that something good would happen to me today, and finding that twenty-dollar bill proved it!

8. Maria knew she was being _?_ when she asked the famous musician to listen to a tape of her songs.

9. Almost every year, the same two teams _?_ for the championship title.

10. Brandon won high marks in the speech competition for impressive _?_ and delivery.

IV. IMPROVING WRITING SKILLS

Exercise A

Maya Angelou makes extensive use of comparisons in "Graduation." These comparisons startle readers into awareness and help us imagine a scene more vividly.

Angelou employs both *similes* and *metaphors* in her writing. A simile is a comparison between two essentially unlike things that uses the words "as" or "like." "Years of withdrawal were brushed aside and left behind, as hanging ropes of parasitic moss" is one such example of a simile in Angelou's story.

A metaphor makes a direct comparison and does not use "as" or "like." "The ugliness they left was palpable. An uninvited guest who wouldn't leave" is an excellent example from "Graduation."

Angelou also uses more developed comparisons that sometimes involve figurative language and sometimes do not. Her discussion of the differences between the graduates and the rest of the students or her contrast of black and white graduates are instances of lengthy comparisons.

Now try imitating Angelou's example by using comparisons to describe an important school event or family celebration. Before you begin writing, create some similes and metaphors to make your description more vivid. Then work these comparisons into your description.

Exercise B

Angelou's "Graduation" is largely auto-bio-graphical. In her work, Angelou demonstrates what most good autobiographers know: The success of an autobiography is not merely mea-sured in terms of how many details an author gives about his or her life. The author also must make personal experiences vivid, appeal-ing, and relevant to readers.

For example, "Graduation" provides many details about a typically significant event. But more important is what Marguerite (Angelou's alter ego) feels and learns during that event. The intense emotions Marguerite experiences will, in most cases, elicit a strong response from readers.

Explore the art of autobiography by writing about an event from your own life. Try to pick an event that others might relate to. Use language that will appeal to your audience's experiences, emotions, and understanding. When you are finished writing and revising, have a partner read your essay and comment about how it affected him or her.

V. THINGS TO WRITE OR TALK ABOUT

1. "Graduation" is just one chapter from Angelou's *I Know Why the Caged Bird Sings*. Read another chapter from her autobiography. Describe Angelou's tone in the two chapters. How does it differ? Does the impression you form of Marguerite differ? Of the two chapters, which did you enjoy the most? Explain.

2. Angelou ends her narrative with this comment on black poets: "Who will compute the lonely nights made less lonely by your songs, or by the empty pots made less tragic by your tales?" What does she mean by this remark? Select another black author and read two or three short selections. (Possible authors include

James Baldwin, Gwendolyn Brooks, Langston Hughes, Alice Walker, Jean Toomer, Toni Morrison, and Henry Dumas.) How does Angelou's comment apply to this author's work? Explain.

3. When speaking of her writing, Angelou has said, "I speak to the black experience, but I am always talking about the human condition." What black experiences are addressed in the selection? What aspects of the universal human condition are discussed? Which do you think Angelou stresses in "Graduation": the black experience or the human condition? Explain.

4. Angelou uses a literary allusion (or reference) when she refers to Patrick Henry. Why is this allusion appropriate? What other allusions can be found in the selection? How does Angelou use these allusions to convey her message?

5. Graduation is usually considered a time of maturing and new beginnings. What signs of maturity does Marguerite show before the graduation ceremonies? How does she mature as a result of her graduation experience? At the end of the selection, what new beginning does Marguerite's life promise?

ANSWER KEY

I. THE STORY LINE

A. Digging for Facts

1. c	3. c	5. a	7. a	9. a
2. a	4. b	6. b	8. c	10. a

B. Probing for Theme

1. Freedom begins with pride in the heart.

III. DEVELOPING WORD POWER

Exercise A

1. mollified
   d. soothed
2. vied
   b. competed
3. presumptuous
   a. overbold
4. constrained
   a. repressed
5. presentiment
   c. expectation

Exercise B

1. (i) purported
2. (f) piqued
3. (c) meticulous
4. (e) palpable
5. (a) constrained
6. (d) mollified
7. (g) presentiment
8. (h) presumptuous
9. (j) vied
10. (b) elocution